God's Law of Adjustment

The Christian Science Publishing Society
One Norway Street, Boston, Massachusetts 02115 U.S.A.

God's Law of Adjustment

ISBN-13: 978-0-87510-413-3
ISBN-10: 0-87510-413-4

Printed in USA

Table of Contents

God's Law of Adjustment

Man lives by divine decree. He is created, governed, supported, and controlled in accord with the law of God. Law means or implies a rule that is established and maintained by power; that which possesses permanence and stability; that which is unchanging, unyielding, and continuous—"the same yesterday, and to-day, and for ever."[1] The efficiency of law rests entirely in the power that enforces it. A law (so called) that is incapable of being enforced is not law and bears no relationship to law. God is the only creator, the only lawmaker. "All things were made by him; and without him was not any thing made that was made."[2] All the power, action, intelligence, life, and government in the universe belong to God and have always belonged to Him. He is the Supreme Ruler and does not share His power with another.

Paul said, "The law of the Spirit of life in Christ

Jesus hath made me free from the law of sin and death."[3] So too we know that "the law of the Spirit of life" frees us from "the law of sin and death." Why? Because all the power there is, is on the side of the law of Life, and that which is opposed to this law of Life is not law at all; it is only belief. In other words, every law of God has behind it infinite power to enforce it, while the so-called law of sin and death has no foundation, has nothing back of it that it can depend upon.

When we understandingly declare that the law of God is present and is in operation, we have invoked or brought into action the whole law and the power of God. We have declared the truth, God's truth—and that truth of God is the law of annihilation, obliteration, and elimination to everything that is unlike Him. When we have stated this truth, and applied it, as taught in Christian Science, to any discordant belief with which we are confronted, we have done all that we can do and all that is necessary for us to do in the destruction of any manifestation of error that ever claimed to exist. Error, which has no place in divine Mind, claims to exist in human thought. When we have put it out of human thought, we have driven it out of the only place where it ever pretended to have a foothold, and thereafter to us it becomes nothing.

There is a law of God that is applicable to every conceivable phase of human experience, and no situation or condition can present itself to mortal thought which can possibly exist outside of the direct influence of this infinite law. The effect of the operation of law is always to correct and govern, to harmonize and adjust. Whatever is out of order or discordant can have no basic Principle of its own, but must come under the direct government of God through what may be termed God's law of adjustment. We are not responsible for the carrying out of this law. In fact, we can do nothing in any way to increase, stimulate, or intensify the action or operation of divine Mind, since it is constantly present, always operative, and never ceases to assert and declare itself when rightly appealed to. All we have to do is scientifically to bring this law of adjustment into contact with our unfinished problem, and when we have done this we have performed our full duty. Someone may say, "How can the law of God, operating mentally, affect my problem, which is physical?" This is easily understood when it is realized that the problem is not physical but mental. First we must know that all is Mind and that there is no such thing as matter, and thus exclude from thought the offending material sense.

The original definition of the word "disease" is lack of ease—discomfort, uneasiness, trouble, disquiet, annoyance, injury. "Disease," says Mary Baker Eddy, the Discoverer and Founder of Christian Science, "is an image of thought externalized. The mental state is called a material state. Whatever is cherished in mortal mind as the physical condition is imaged forth on the body." [4] This also applies to heat, cold, hunger, poverty, or any form of discord, all of which are mental, though mortal mind regards them as material states. It can therefore be easily seen how the law of God, which is mental, can be applied to a physical problem.

In reality, the problem is not physical, but purely mental, and is the direct result of some thought cherished in mortal mind. If a man were drowning in mid-ocean with apparently no human help at hand, there is a law of God which, when rightly appealed to, would bring about his rescue. Does the reader doubt this? Then he must believe that it is possible for man to find himself in a condition where God cannot help him. If one were in a burning building or a railroad accident, or if he were in a den of lions, there is a law of God which could at once adjust the apparent material circumstances so as to bring about his complete deliverance.

It is not necessary for us to know in each individual case just what this law of God is, nor how it is going to operate, and an attempted investigation into the why and wherefore might only serve to interfere with its operation and hinder the demonstration. Any fear on our part, occasioned by the fact that divine Mind does not know of our plight, or that infinite wisdom lacks the intelligence necessary to bring about a rescue, should be instantly put out of thought. In *Science and Health with Key to the Scriptures,* Mrs. Eddy writes, "The divine Mind, which forms the bud and blossom, will care for the human body, even as it clothes the lily; but let no mortal interfere with God's government by thrusting in the laws of erring, human concepts."[5] The trouble with us usually is that we want to know just how God is going to help us and when the good results are to be experienced; then we will pass judgment upon it and decide whether we are ready to trust our case in His hands.

Let us see, then, where God's law of adjustment operates. God has no need of being adjusted. The only place where there is any demand for adjustment is in human consciousness; but unless human consciousness appeals to the divine law, unless it is willing and ready to lay down its own sense of human will and stop human planning, put aside human pride, ambition, and vanity, there is no room for the law of adjustment to operate.

When we in our helplessness reach the point where we see we are unable of ourselves to do anything, and then call upon God to aid us; when we are ready to show our willingness to abandon our own plans, our own opinions, our own sense of what ought to be done under the circumstances, and have no fear as to the consequences—then God's law will take possession of and govern the whole situation. We cannot expect, however, that this law will operate in our behalf if we indulge any preconceived ideas as to how it should do its work. We must completely abandon our own view of things and say, "Not my will, but thine, be done."[6] If this step is taken with confidence and a full trust that God is capable of taking care of every circumstance, then no power on earth can prevent the natural, rightful, and legitimate adjustment of all discordant conditions.

This law of adjustment is the universal law of Love, which bestows its blessings on all alike. It does not take from one and give to another. It does not withhold itself under any circumstances, but is ready, and waiting to operate as soon as the invitation is given and human will is set aside. "Whatever holds human thought in line with unselfed love," our Leader says, "receives directly the divine power."[7] When we reach the point where we can in confidence and in trust leave everything to the settlement of

God's law of adjustment, it will immediately relieve us of all sense of personal responsibility, remove anxiety and fear, and bring peace, comfort, and the assurance of God's protecting care.

The most satisfying and comforting sense of peace and joy always follows the willingness on our part to allow God to control every situation for us through His law of adjustment. When we understand that infinite Mind is the Ruler of the universe, that every idea of God is forever in its proper place, that no condition or circumstance can arise whereby a mistake can find lodgment in God's plan, then we have the complete assurance that God is capable of adjusting everything as it should be. The fact is that all things are already in their rightful place; that no interference or lack of adjustment can really occur. It is only to the unenlightened human sense that there can be any such thing as discord. God's universe is always in perfect adjustment, and all His ideas work together forever in perfect harmony.

When we are willing to give up our frightened and uncertain sense of things and let the divine Mind govern, then and then only shall we behold that "all things work together for good to them that love God."[8] The discord which seems to be apparent is only what mortal mind believes, whether it be sickness, discomfort, annoyance, or trouble of any kind. When we are willing to relinquish our present views, even though we may believe we are in the right and another in the wrong, we shall not suffer by laying down our human opinions, but rather find that the law of God is ready and active in the right adjustment of everything involved. It may sometimes seem hard when we feel that we are oppressed or imposed upon, to stop resisting, but if our faith in the power of Truth to adjust all things is sufficient, we should be glad of the opportunity to relinquish our claims and place our trust in infinite wisdom, which will adjust everything according to its own unerring law. There is no such thing as failure in the divine Mind. God is never defeated, and those who stand with Him will always receive the benefits of a victory over error.

What then are we to do when we find ourselves involved in a controversy, in a dispute, or in an unpleasant situation of any kind? What are we to do when we have been attacked and maligned, misrepresented or abused? Should we endeavor to return in kind what has been done to us? This would not be appealing to God's law of adjustment. So long as we endeavor to settle the difficulty ourselves, we are interfering with the action of the law of God. Under any circumstance of this kind it will avail us nothing to fight back. We simply show our human weakness when we take the matter into our own hands and attempt either to punish our enemies or to extricate ourselves through any virtue of our own.

When there seem to be two ways of working out a problem in business or in any of the various walks of life, and we decide on a way which seems best, how can we tell, when there are so many arguments against that way, whether the decision is based on Truth or error? Here is a question which can be decided only through the demonstration of God's law of adjustment. There are times when human wisdom is inadequate to tell us just what is the right thing to be done. Under such circumstances we should pray humbly for divine guidance, and then choose that which seems to be in accord with our highest sense of right, knowing that God's law of adjustment regulates and governs all things; and even if we choose the wrong way, we as Christian Scientists have a right to know that God will not allow us to continue in a mistake, but will show us the right way and compel us to walk therein.

When we have reached the point where we are willing to do what seems to us the best and then leave the problem with God, knowing that He will adjust everything according to His unchanging law, we can then withdraw ourselves entirely from the proposition, drop all sense of responsibility, and feel secure in the knowledge that God corrects and governs all things righteously. All we ever need to do is that which is pleasing in the sight of God, that which conforms to divine requirements. If our good is evilly spoken of, this does not affect the situation in any degree, since God does not hold us accountable for the action of others. Our responsibility ceases when we have complied with the demands of good, and there we can afford to let any question rest. It makes no difference how much is at stake or what is involved, if we succeed in getting ourselves out of the way, we can then be satisfied with the words of the prophet: "...the battle is not yours, but God's. ... set yourselves, stand ye still, and see the salvation of the Lord."[9]

We cannot hope to work out of this human sense of existence without making mistakes. We may make many, but will profit by them all. We are at liberty to change our belief of things as often as we get new light. We should not let our vanity compel us to adhere to a proposition simply because we have taken a stand thereon. We should be willing to relinquish our former views and change our thought on any subject as often as wisdom furnishes us enlightenment.

Christian Scientists are sometimes accused of being changeable. What if they are, if it is always

God that changes them? Is a Christian Scientist any less a Scientist because he changes his mind? Is a general less fit to lead his army because in the heat of battle he changes his tactics under the guidance of wisdom? A too determined sense of carrying out a preconceived plan is more likely to be the enthronement of erring human will.

Christian Scientists are minutemen, armed and equipped to respond to any call of wisdom, always ready and willing to abandon personal views or opinions, and to allow that Mind to be in them "which was also in Christ Jesus." [10]

— *Adam H. Dickey*

Originally published in the January 1916 issue of *The Christian Science Journal*.

1. Hebrews 13:8
2. John 1:3
3. Romans 8:2
4. Mary Baker Eddy, *Science and Health with Key to the Scriptures*, p. 411
5. Eddy, *Science and Health*, p. 62
6. Luke 22:42
7. Eddy, *Science and Health*, p. 192
8. Romans 8:28
9. II Chronicles 20:15, 17
10. Philippians 2:5

Testimony of Healing

On December 12, 1943, the first really cold day of the winter, I was working at my wartime job as a shipfitter at New England's largest shipyard. For several days I had been installing "swash lids" on the fuel tanks of a large combat vessel. The fuel tanks of warships are scattered along the bottom of the hull, occupying space not utilized for other purposes, and separated from one another by bulkheads which are watertight and fireproof.

The most difficult and tiring part of my work resulted from this method of placement, as it necessitated much crawling through cramped areas and numberless small openings known as "escape holes." I had to pull an electric welding line over one hundred feet long to the many compartments where lids were required, to carry a welder's shield, an extension electric light cord, and a tool bag.

On this particular day I thought I was going to finish the assignment by installing the last of thirty-nine lids, only to find when checking my work list that somewhere I had missed one tank. This was very discouraging, for, numb with cold from lying on the frigid steel, I was anxious to get through and do some other work that would allow me to stand up and move about.

I was tempted to leave the one lid undone and let someone else do it when it was found incomplete. However, it was my habit to complete my assignments before asking for another job. So I explored the whole ship's bottom and found that the tank I had missed was the one I should have done first, situated way up forward near the bow of the vessel.

I started installing the lid, which necessitated my getting inside the tank through the "escape hole," an opening of fifteen by twenty-three inches, because the "swash lids" open downward into the tanks.

I had to weld the hinge on which the lid swung to the interior of the tank and to the lid. In order to locate the hinge correctly and to allow the lid to swing freely when opening and closing I had been instructed always to bolt the lid in place with the thirty-six bolts required to hold it and then weld on the hinge.

I tried to put the first bolt in place while holding the lid on top of my head with one hand, but I was so numb with cold, and so tired from crawling so far with my equipment, that I could not accomplish this simple act until the eighth attempt. Finally, the threads of the first bolt caught and I soon had enough bolts to hold the lid in place. Then when I looked for my wrench to tighten the bolts, I discovered that somewhere along the way I had dropped it. I was faced with the choice of taking the lid down and crawling back through the inner-bottom of the ship until I found my wrench or going ahead with the work by tightening the bolts as much as I could with my fingers and welding the hinge on. I decided on the latter course.

When the welding was finished and I was ready to leave, satisfied the work was properly done, I found that the bolts I had put on with my fingers would not come out. The welding had caused a distortion of the steel which had added a strain somewhere and I was a prisoner by my own hand.

Instantly sensing the seriousness of my position, I realized I had to demonstrate for myself the truths I had so often professed. Many aggressive mental suggestions came to my consciousness.

I met each one with its counterfact. The first scientific thought that came to me was the subject of the Lesson-Sermon to be read in all Christian Science churches the next day, "God the Preserver of Man."

I never let go of that one fact and I worked as I had been taught. When Satan whispered, "You're alone and no help will come," I knew that God was infinite, ever present, and that therefore I was not alone. Again the whisper came: "It's four degrees above zero and it's now Saturday noon. If you don't get out by three o'clock you will be here until seven o'clock Monday morning. Do you think you'll survive?" Then the truth came to my consciousness: "God is your Life; you cannot die."

A fierce mental battle was fought in my consciousness, inside that cold tank. It was not ended easily or very rapidly. Aggressive mental suggestions sought to gain control over me by fear. But, thank God, I knew the counterfacts of every lie.

All the while I was striving to twist the bolts out with my fingers, working at one then another to find one I could move. Picking up my electric light to examine the bolts I saw threads of flesh clinging to the heads of the bolts. Looking at my fingers, I saw the torn flesh. I had felt no pain. My fear of imprisonment was greater than my sense of pain and overshadowed it.

The devil prompted me to scream, to pound on the steel, to seek another opening, to use my welding rod to burn the bolts off. But I knew that no one could hear. Rivet guns were roaring down aft somewhere on the hull. I started to crawl into the other compartment of the tank, but my fear of leaving the comfort of my electric light, and the knowledge that there was no other escape hole, put an end to that temptation. Wisdom told me: "You have never tried burning a bolt away. It has been done, but you don't know how. If you fail to burn it through and add weld to the bolt you'll be welded in."

I was still striving to twist the bolts out. It finally came to me that I must stop my human efforts and trust wholly in God. It required an actual physical effort to take my hands away from the bolts. But I finally put them down in my lap, and then I spoke to God. I said, "God, I'm listening." The change was wonderful. A message from an article written by Adam H. Dickey entitled, "God's Law of Adjustment," came to me. The statement was, "If a man were drowning in mid-ocean with apparently no human help at hand, there is a law of God which, when rightly appealed to, would bring about his rescue."

With this thought came absolute calmness, a sense of peace, a certainty of God's nearness, a positive assurance of deliverance. I waited and heard the direction, "Take out the pin in the hinge." Even as I moved to obey, the dark angel said: "What good will that do? The bolts hold the lid, not the hinge." But there was no contest. I knew the voice that I would follow.

I removed the pin from the hinge, dropped my hands into my lap, and waited. Again the voice came: "Take out the bolt at the left." My fingers grasped the bolt at the left and strained to twist it. It moved. I took a new hold, putting my whole effort into keeping it turning until it came free. I continued removing one bolt after another until only one remained that I could not move.

Again I dropped my hands to my lap and waited. The words of a much loved hymn can best describe the amazement I felt as I saw my deliverance working out step by step,

> "I was not ever thus, nor prayed that Thou
> Shouldst lead me on;
> I loved to choose and see my path; but now
> Lead Thou me on." [1]

The angel voice said, "Pull down on the lid." The lid bent as I pulled with all my strength so the hole was partly open. The impulse came to try to wedge my way through. But the right thought came in time: "Don't try that; you will get caught part way and be unable to go ahead or back. Pull down again." This time there was more than the strength of muscles. The threads were stripped from the bolt and the lid crashed into my lap. I was free! Looking out into the dark inner bottom of the ship, I saw my welding line and extension electric light cord winding back the way I must go to get to the "escape trunk" and then up to the deck of the ship. I had felt the need to see that the way was unobstructed.

Then I sat back in the tank and silently praised God, rejoicing that Christian Science had given such power to men. I reviewed my many blessings and counted not least among them the class instruction I had received. My gratitude to Mrs. Eddy was profound and beyond words.

I installed the lid properly on the hinge and left the ship. When I arrived home my wife met me and said, "I have been working all day for you to come home safely." She had felt my need, and supplied it by right knowing and persistent declarations of the truth about man. I was so overcome with gratitude that it was hours before I could speak of what had occurred.

No other experience has given me the sense of nearness to God that I gained from this one. I felt His presence and followed His angels' voices. I believe I have learned to recognize divine guidance.

— *Roland H. Allen*
West Newton, Massachusetts, USA

- -

Originally published in the June 2, 1945,
issue of the *Christian Science Sentinel.*

[1] John Henry Newman, *Christian Science Hymnal*, No. 169

The ideas expressed in this collection are based
on the teachings of Christian Science, which is fully
explained in the Christian Science textbook,
Science and Health with Key to the Scriptures
by Mary Baker Eddy. For more ideas like the
ones presented in this collection, please visit
www.christianscience.com or the website
of The Church of Christ, Scientist:
www.churchofchristscientist.org